Sabbath Rest

Disciplines of Devotion

Edited by Winfree Brisley

Fasting, by Cassie Achermann

Prayer, by Courtney Reissig

Sabbath Rest, by Megan Hill

Sabbath Rest

Megan Hill

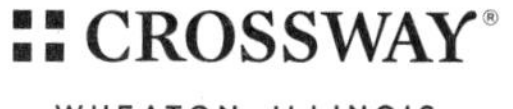

WHEATON, ILLINOIS

Sabbath Rest

Published by Crossway
1300 Crescent Street
Wheaton, Illinois 60187

Cover design: David Fassett

Cover image: Getty Images and Rawpixel

First printing 2026

Printed in the United States of America

Trade paperback ISBN: 978-1-4335-9956-9
ePub ISBN: 978-1-4335-9958-3
PDF ISBN: 978-1-4335-9957-6

Library of Congress Cataloging-in-Publication Data

Names: Hill, Megan, 1978– author.
Title: Sabbath rest / Megan Hill.
Description: Wheaton, Illinois : Crossway, 2026 | Series: Disciplines of devotion | Includes bibliographical references.
Identifiers: LCCN 2025003250 (print) | LCCN 2025003251 (ebook) | ISBN 9781433599569 (trade paperback) | ISBN 9781433599576 (pdf) | ISBN 9781433599583 (epub)
Subjects: LCSH: Sunday.
Classification: LCC BV111.3 .H55 2026 (print) | LCC BV111.3 (ebook) | DDC 263/.3—dc23/eng/20250825
LC record available at https://lccn.loc.gov/2025003250
LC ebook record available at https://lccn.loc.gov/2025003251

Crossway is a publishing ministry of Good News Publishers.

BP 35 34 33 32 31 30 29 28 27 26
15 14 13 12 11 10 9 8 7 6 5 4 3 2 1

For Evelyn, child of the covenant.
May you always call the Sabbath a delight (Isa. 58:13).

Contents

Series Preface

ON A CHILLY JANUARY MORNING, two friends and I huddled around a coffee shop table to share life updates and prayer requests. One friend reflected on the previous year with frustration: "I feel like I didn't accomplish anything." The other friend and I, surprised by her assessment, rattled off a long list of worthwhile things she had done. But she persisted. It wasn't that she truly believed she had accomplished nothing; it was that the things she had done weren't the things she had hoped to do. Things she valued had been pushed aside by what seemed more urgent in the moment.

I could say the same, and I bet you could too. As women living in a do-it-all culture, we tend to have a lot on our plates. We juggle work, husbands, children, aging parents, and friends. We manage households, serve in the church, and volunteer in the community. Year after year, many of our goals and good intentions get pushed to the back burner—especially when it comes to spiritual growth.

We want to grow in relationship with the Lord. We want to know the Bible better, fight sin, and establish a consistent prayer life. But amid all the things we have to do, we often miss the one thing we really need. In Psalm 27:4 David said,

> One thing have I asked of the Lord,
>   that will I seek after:
> that I may dwell in the house of the Lord
>   all the days of my life,
> to gaze upon the beauty of the Lord
>   and to inquire in his temple.

As king, David surely had many things to do and many things he might have asked of God. But he knew that what he most needed was to dwell with the Lord. Similarly, Jesus explained to Martha in Luke 10:41–42 that she was "anxious and troubled about many things, but one thing is necessary." What was the one thing? Sitting at his feet, listening to his teaching.

As you consider your relationship with the Lord, are you more like David or Martha? Are you *devoted* or *distracted*? I suspect that many of us would admit that we identify with Martha's distraction but also long for David's devotion. So how can we grow in devotion to God in a world of endless distractions?

We see from both David and Martha that a life devoted to the Lord won't happen by accident. David resolved to seek after God's presence. Jesus suggested that Martha needed to sit down and listen. You see, discipline helps us grow in devotion.

In fact, throughout history Christians have used spiritual disciplines such as prayer, fasting, and Bible study to seek the Lord and grow in relationship with him. If the phrase "spiritual disciplines" sounds intimidating, don't worry! It simply means practices that promote spiritual growth.[1] And these practices can help you draw near to God whether you're a new believer or have been walking with the Lord for decades.

Perhaps the idea of cultivating a life of devotion to the Lord is new or confusing, and you don't know where to start. You have faith in Christ, but you're trying to figure out what it looks like to grow in relationship with him.

Or maybe you're going through the motions of spending time with God, but if you're honest, he feels distant. You want the Holy Spirit to warm your affections for the things of God and restore the joy of your salvation.

Or perhaps you have a vibrant relationship with the Lord, but you'd like to learn new ways to seek him. You've been wanting to try fasting or you'd like to learn about Sabbath rest.

Whatever your situation, the Disciplines of Devotion series was written for you. Each booklet explores

1 Donald S. Whitney, *Spiritual Disciplines for the Christian Life* (NavPress, 1991), 17.

one thing—one practice to cultivate, one spiritual discipline to grow in—to help you draw near to the one true God. In each booklet, you'll gain a biblical understanding of a particular discipline and why it's worth cultivating. And you'll explore three practical ways to get started.

If you'd like to grow in these disciplines alongside other believers, we've included reflection questions to facilitate group discussion. Consider using this series in one-on-one discipleship, with a group of teens, in a neighborhood Bible study, or with a church small group. Also, Christians have a variety of perspectives on these disciplines, so if you'd like to continue your personal study, you can find a list of recommended resources at the end of each booklet.

When you finish this volume, let me encourage you not to set it aside in a pile of good intentions. These booklets can be read in less than an hour, but the disciplines they recommend can help you seek the Lord for a lifetime—even as you go about all the things you have to do.

Preaching about the "one thing" David desired in Psalm 27:4, Scottish pastor Alexander Maclaren observed, "Most of us seem, to our own consciousness, to live amidst endless distractions all our days. . . . But if we are true to the one purpose of serving and keeping near God, then we have a charm against the frittering away of our lives in distractions."[2]

The Disciplines of Devotion series isn't about productivity or efficiency or doing less. It's about pursuing a life of devotion to the Lord in an age of endless distraction. It's an invitation to "taste and see that the LORD is good!" (Ps. 34:8) no matter how much is on your plate.

Winfree Brisley
SERIES EDITOR

2 Alexander Maclaren, *Expositions of Holy Scripture: Psalms* (Eerdmans, 1932), 146.

1

What Is Sabbath Rest?

EVERYONE I KNOW is longing for rest. The teenagers in my life are worn out with studying, extracurriculars, and relational drama. The moms and grandmas are juggling everyone's schedules while squeezing their own tasks into the margins. My coworkers are putting in extra time and marking the days until the next paid holiday. Our alarms get us up early, our to-do lists keep us up late, and each week brings a fresh set of urgent responsibilities. We are tired. The psalmist didn't have text messaging or video calls or car repairs, but he knew the same sense of weariness that we do. "It is in vain that you rise up early and go late to rest," he wrote, "eating the bread of anxious toil" (Ps. 127:2). The must-dos and have-tos of life in 900 BC were just as pressing as they are in our day. But, he continued, the Lord "gives to his beloved sleep" (v. 2).

In a lifetime of "anxious toil," we need a regular reset. Day after day, the tasks just keep coming, and while the Bible affirms the goodness of work, it also acknowledges its frustrations. "In vain" you fold the laundry and do the dishes, only to face a new pile tomorrow. "In vain" you schedule appointments and meet deadlines, only to confront an overflowing inbox next week. We need rest. Thankfully, the psalmist knew where to find it. It's a gift from "the Lord" (v. 1). And it's a gift particularly to his people, "his beloved" (v. 2), the ones he has redeemed. As God's people, we look to the Lord to establish our work and relationships (vv. 1, 3–5), and we look to him to give us periods of rest (v. 2).

So where can we sign up for regular rest from the hand of our gracious God? Where do we receive this gift? We receive it in the Sabbath.

Psalm 127 isn't merely a song about the daily grind and our biological need for eight hours of sleep every night. That's a tune our unbelieving neighbors could sing without regard for the Lord. Psalm 127 is a psalm of ascent, one of the songs Old Testament believers would sing together on their way to worship. These lines about yielding our labor to the Lord and looking to him for refreshment echo the pattern of the Sabbath. They're about more than sleep for the body; they're about respite for the soul.

Leave your anxious toil, beloved ones, and enjoy God's Sabbath rest.

Sabbath's Foundations

The word *Sabbath* may sound curiously old-fashioned. Maybe it's a word you associate only with Moses's Ten Commandments or with laws governing colonial New England. It may seem like a hopelessly dated idea or a harshly Pharisaical one. But *Sabbath* appears throughout both the Old and New Testaments, and Sabbath observance continues to be practiced by believers throughout the world today.

What's more, the Bible consistently presents the Sabbath as the Lord's gift to the weary.

Simply defined, the Sabbath is one day each week that God sets aside for his redeemed people to rest from their daily work in order to worship and enjoy him.

To understand the Sabbath and how the Lord would have us observe it, we need to turn to Scripture. In a brief survey of key passages in the Bible, we'll see that the priority of the Sabbath stretches throughout the story of redemption, from the beginning of time all the way into our eternal future.

Creation (Gen. 2:1–3)

The Christian practice of Sabbath rest has foundations that were laid long before our days of smartphones and remote work. They were laid before the time of Christ and before the time of Moses. They were laid even before "thorns and thistles" sprang up to make our work in a fallen world more toilsome and less rewarding (Gen. 3:18). Sabbath rest has its foundations in creation.

On the seventh day of creation, "God finished his work that he had done, and he rested . . . from all his work that he had done" (Gen. 2:2). Having created the world and everything in it, God rested. And he established that day of rest as a sacred day of blessing going forward: "God blessed the Sabbath day and made it holy, because on it God rested from all his work that he had done in creation" (v. 3). Beginning with the first Sabbath in the history of the world, God and all his creation enjoyed holy rest.

Manna (Ex. 16)

In the wilderness, too, God's people observed the Sabbath. They looked to him to order their work, their worship, and their time. He graciously provided food for them—"bread from heaven"—that they only had to collect and eat (Ex. 16:4). But even the minimal labor of scooping bread into baskets had God-given boundaries of rest: " 'Six days you shall gather it, but on the seventh day, which is a Sabbath, there will be none.' . . . So the people rested on the seventh day" (vv. 26, 30). After creation and even before the law of Moses, God gave his people "a day of solemn rest" (v. 23).

Mosaic Law (Ex. 20:8–11; 31:12–17; Deut. 5:12–15)

At Sinai, when God wrote his law in stone, one of his commandments concerned rest and worship on the Sabbath: "Remember the Sabbath day, to keep it holy" (Ex. 20:8; cf. Deut. 5:12–15). This commandment has both positive and negative aspects. The people were to "remember" and "keep" the day, doing "all [their] work" on the other days, and they were to "not do any work" and require no work from others on the Sabbath (vv. 8–10). Later, the Lord expanded on his Sabbath command and called it "a covenant forever" for his people to observe "throughout their generations" (Ex. 31:16). Because of the pattern of the Lord's own day of rest at creation (Ex. 20:11), God's people rest individually and corporately on the Sabbath from their daily work. As Christopher Watkin explains, "God's rest [at creation] makes it clear that work is not all there is for God, and we know from Exodus 20 that he doesn't want it to be all there is for us either."[1]

Prophets (Isa. 58:13–14)

The prophets regularly speak about the Sabbath, and Isaiah has one of the most beautiful pictures of the Sabbath in all Scripture. Writing to a people snared by sin and threatened by their enemies, he offered them the joy of God's rest:

> If you turn back your foot from the Sabbath,
> from doing your pleasure on my holy day,
> and call the Sabbath a delight
> and the holy day of the LORD honorable;
> if you honor it, not going your own ways,
> or seeking your own pleasure, or talking idly;
> then you shall take delight in the LORD,
> and I will make you ride on the heights of
> the earth. (Isa. 58:13–14)

1 Christopher Watkin, *Biblical Critical Theory: How the Bible's Unfolding Story Makes Sense of Modern Life and Culture* (Zondervan Academic, 2022), 79.

Sabbath rest is ordained by God ("my holy day"), directed by God ("not going your own ways"), and blessed by God ("you shall take delight"). When God's people honor him on this day, he refreshes their souls, making them "ride on the heights of the earth."

Jesus (Matt. 12:1–14; Mark 2:23–3:6; Luke 14:1–6; John 5:1–17)

Sabbath rest isn't just an Old Testament practice. In his earthly ministry, Jesus honored the Sabbath day, resting from his daily work and prioritizing corporate worship (Luke 4:16), and his disciples did too (Luke 23:56). He did God's will on the Sabbath, healing and feeding people and ministering to their souls (Matt. 12:1–14; Mark 2:23–3:6; John 5:1–17). He affirmed the Sabbath's goodness (Mark 2:27). Additionally, he declared his identity as God by calling himself "lord of the Sabbath" (Matt. 12:8). Jesus's practice of the Sabbath was perfect, and we honor and imitate him when we delight in the day he made for us.

New Testament Church (Acts 20:7; 1 Cor. 16:2; Rev. 1:10)

With Christ's resurrection on the first day of the week, the Sabbath experienced a shift. Old Testament believers set apart the seventh day, shaping their week in light of creation; New Testament believers set apart the first day, shaping their week in light of the resurrection. "The first day of every week" (1 Cor. 16:2; cf. Acts 20:7) became the day of fellowship and worship—the Christian Sabbath—for God's new covenant people. Even the apostle John, exiled on the island of Patmos, observed the Sabbath. He received his vision of the things to come when he set aside his ordinary tasks and was "in the Spirit on the Lord's day" (Rev. 1:10). As God's people celebrate Christ's resurrection and honor his day, we receive his presence and blessing.

Sabbath's Future

Sabbath rest is part of our weekly life now, and it will characterize our life in eternity too. In fact, our practice of Sabbath on this earth anticipates and prepares for the Sabbath to come. The author of Hebrews connects the Old Testament Sabbath with our Sabbath observance today and then points ultimately to the Sabbath rest of heaven (Heb. 4:1–13). In the new heavens and earth, believers "rest from their labors, for their deeds follow them!" (Rev. 14:13).

The trajectory of Scripture is not that the Sabbath becomes less important through redemptive history. Rather, it becomes increasingly more important until eventually it becomes all there is—that great, eternal Sabbath rest when God's people will gather in their Lord's near presence, cease all their earthly work, and worship him forever (Rev. 7:9–12).

Reflection Questions

1. What has been your past experience with Sabbath rest? Why are you interested in growing in this discipline?

2. Read one of the Scripture passages discussed in this chapter. How does this passage add to your understanding of Sabbath rest?

2

What Are the Blessings of Sabbath Rest?

I'VE BEEN PRACTICING Sabbath rest since I was a child. For my younger self—a small human without work obligations—Sabbath rest was a long, happy day of seeing church friends, singing loud in worship, and eating tasty food. In later years, I began to appreciate being called to set aside my work—first schoolwork and later my employment and household tasks—to focus on Christ and receive his gifts. Over more than two thousand Sundays, I've worshiped with the church, memorized Scripture, feasted with God's people, ministered to the saints, and wrestled with the Lord in prayer.

By now, setting apart one day each week to worship and enjoy the Lord is a habit. No other practice has been better for my soul.

The Sabbath may be a day of rest, but it doesn't come easily. When we try it, we quickly realize we live in a world that isn't oriented toward rest—or toward the God who gives rest. Particularly in contemporary America, with its expectations of constant availability, we work more and rest less than we ever have.[1] What's more, in any age, our hearts prefer to tackle the demands in front of our faces rather than seek the Lord in the invisible places (Matt. 6:31–32). It's often easier to start another load of laundry than to sit down and pray.

In his book *Rest*, researcher Alex Soojung-Kim Pang writes, "Rest doesn't just magically appear when we need it, especially in today's busy world. Taking

1 Alex Soojung-Kim Pang, *Rest: Why You Get More Done When You Work Less* (Basic Books, 2018), 2.

rest seriously requires recognizing its importance . . . and carving out and defending space for rest in our daily lives."[2] It's not effortless to rest, but when we make it a priority, Pang observes, we have the space to consider our lives and reorient ourselves to what's important.[3]

Believers can appreciate that Pang is onto something. We need to take rest seriously. The Sabbath is the pattern God established from Genesis to Revelation, so we ought to recognize this pattern and defend it in our lives. The Lord invites us to set aside ordinary things and experience the blessing of spiritual things. Let's consider five ways Sabbath rest reorients us toward what matters most.

Sabbath Rest Reorients Our Time

As tempting as it might be to believe that we're masters of our time, carefully manipulating a complex puzzle of Google calendar entries, we aren't. God is the one who created time, who set us in it and bound

2 Pang, *Rest*, 240–41.

3 Pang, *Rest*, 241–42.

us by it, and God is the one who rightfully directs us how to use it. When we submit to his pattern of six days for work and one for worship, we acknowledge that God is the Lord of time.

The disruption of Sabbath rest is a chance to remember that even our schedules are under the Lord's authority. Once a week, the Lord breaks into our routines and reminds us that our appointments and plans are not ultimate, nor are they prioritized according to *our* desires. When the first day of every week belongs wholly to him, it reorients every minute of every day that follows.[4]

Sabbath Rest Reorients Our Work

I love a to-do list. In fact, I've been known to complete a task and then add it to my to-do list merely for the pleasure of crossing it off immediately. I measure the success of each day by how many items have a dark slash through them. Phone meeting? Done.

4 Parts of this section are adapted from my article "Are Sundays Good for Babies?," The Gospel Coalition, February 24, 2019, https://www.thegospelcoalition.org/. Used by permission.

Pick up prescriptions? Done. Order groceries? Done. Submit project? Done. Satisfied by my labors, I go to bed happy.

Except on Sundays. On Sunday nights, I have to reckon with the fact that I accomplished very little. I didn't clock in to my job or run any errands. I have *less* money in my bank account, having left some in the offering plate. I've completed no assignments that I can cross off my list and congratulate myself with. But guess what? I had food in my stomach and breath in my lungs; the sun continued to shine, and the earth continued to turn. I did nothing, and the Lord did everything.

We're often tempted to think our effort is what keeps us afloat, but Sabbath rest reminds us that it's the Lord who gives us daily bread, who provides our clothing, and who supplies a place for us to live (Matt. 6:11, 25–30). Even more importantly, Sabbath rest reminds us that we don't secure any spiritual blessing by our own hands—including our salvation (Heb. 4:1–13). On the cross, Christ did everything, and we did nothing. We begin every week not with labor but with rest, remembering that Christ has already worked for us.

Sabbath Rest Reorients Our Allegiances

Most of us interact with hundreds of people in a given week. We exchange smiles with the mail carrier and texts with a best friend from elementary school. We spend time with classmates, coworkers, neighbors, family members, and acquaintances at the gym. Sabbath rest, however, clarifies whom we are most significantly connected to: the members of Christ's family.

Throughout the week, we make time in our schedules for people who matter to us, but on the Lord's Day, God makes time in our schedules for the people who matter to him. When we gather with the church, we gather with those for whom Christ died. They may not be the people we'd choose for ourselves, but they're the people God has chosen for us. They're the people Scripture calls us to love (John 13:34), greet (Rom. 16:16), know (3 John 15), pray for (James 5:16), serve (Gal. 5:13), forgive

(Col. 3:13), and show hospitality toward (Rom. 12:13). Like me, you probably struggle to do these things in your busy week, but on one whole day, we have the opportunity to live out our commitment to God's people in the church.

Sabbath Rest Reorients Our Priorities

I live in the most secular metropolitan area in America.[5] On Sunday morning, I pass neighbors who are mowing their lawns or are on their morning run. Some of them are loading up their cars with chairs and umbrellas for the beach; others are organizing supplies for a home-improvement project. I've never seen my neighbors headed to church. Their Sunday practices testify to what's important to them: a nice home, a healthy body, time with family. There's nothing wrong with any of those things, but none of them are the most important thing.

Puritan pastor David Clarkson wrote, "The most wonderful things that are now done on earth are

5 "The Most Post-Christian Cities in America: 2019," Barna Group, June 5, 2019, https://www.barna.com/.

wrought in the public ordinances, though the commonness and spiritualness of them makes them seem less wonderful."[6] In other words, what goes on in your church on Sunday may not look like much, but it's the most significant thing happening anywhere in the world. When God's people gather for worship, the Lord promises his presence (Matt. 18:20), proclaims his word (1 Thess. 2:13), receives our prayers and praises (Rev. 5:8), makes us holy (Eph. 5:25–27), converts sinners (Rom. 10:14), and seals us to himself in baptism and the Lord's Supper (Rom. 6:4; 1 Cor. 11:24). Seen through the lens of Scripture, church worship is the pinnacle of every week. Truly, "a day in [the Lord's] courts is better than a thousand elsewhere" (Ps. 84:10).

Without the discipline of Sabbath rest, we can easily take cues from our unbelieving neighbors and squander the day at the soccer field or in front of a screen. The Sabbath, however, invites us to fully engage in the "one thing [that] is necessary" (Luke

6 David Clarkson, "Public Worship to Be Preferred Before Private," in *The Practical Works of David Clarkson* (Edinburgh, 1865), 3:193.

10:42): joining Jesus's disciples and sitting at his feet in worship.

Sabbath Rest Reorients Our Pilgrimage

For several years, I used a planner that had space every month and again every quarter to list big-picture goals for the upcoming weeks. Without those prompts, one day's to-do list rolled into the next. The blank pages functioned as opportunities to stop and consider where I'd been and where I was headed. Similarly, Sabbath rest is a regular nudge for Christian pilgrims: *Stop here and orient yourself. Reflect on your journey. Set your heart on your goal.*

One day a week, we have a chance to take stock of where we've been. *Where have I experienced the Spirit's work? Where have I seen answered prayer? Where have I stumbled into Satan's traps? Where have I grown in grace?* Although we can (and should!) ask these questions as we go through the week, Sabbath rest frees us to step back and consider the big picture. Like Samuel's Ebenezer stone, it prompts us to remember: "Thus far the LORD has helped us" (1 Sam. 7:12 NKJV).

Then, it turns our hearts toward the future. God created us for a greater end than endlessly repeating monotonous tasks. Our earthly work is under a limited contract, and the pause of Sabbath rest reorients us toward that final day when we will rest from all our labors (Rev. 14:13). Weekly, we stop to consider where we've been, and then, refreshed, we again set out toward that holy city where Christ is.

Reflection Questions

1. Consider the five ways Sabbath rest reorients us. Which of these especially highlights a need in your life?

2. Read Exodus 20:8–11. Which parts of this command require us to refrain from doing something? Which parts of this command require us to do something? Are you more likely to think of practicing rest as refraining from something or as actively doing something? Why are both aspects of Sabbath rest important?

3

Prepare to Rest

WHEN I WAS DATING and engaged to my husband Rob, we lived a thousand miles apart. We would see one another only every few months for a couple of days, and it was difficult to squeeze in even those visits. I was an English teacher at a junior high school, and most of my afternoons and evenings were taken up by stacks of eighth-grade essays awaiting my feedback. I'd get up early, go to work, come home, eat something, grab my red pen, and grade until bedtime. The next day, I'd do it all over again. But when Rob was coming to town, my work took on a new urgency. I didn't want to spend his visit holed up in my room, correcting comma splices. I wanted to see him, talk with him, enjoy meals with him. And so, in the days leading up to his arrival, I'd focus on completing as much grading as possible. I'd then catch up on my laundry and purchase groceries for my bare refrigerator. I knew the hours of preparation were worth it because they'd free me up to be with the person I loved.

The first way we practice Sabbath rest doesn't happen on the Sabbath day. To enjoy one day in seven with our soul's beloved, we need to get ready.

How to Get Ready

Consider three ways to prepare, and some practical suggestions.

Prepare Your Work

In one sense, practicing Sabbath rest actually makes *more* work for us—or at least compresses our work into fewer days. As the Lord tells us in the fourth commandment, "Six days you shall labor and do all your work" (Ex. 20:9). God's people in the wilderness went out every day to gather manna, but on the sixth day, they had twice as much work (Ex. 16:5). On that day, they collected and cooked double so they could rest the next day.

For us, too, Sabbath rest means organizing our normal work to fit into the other six days of the week. That might require extra errands on Monday, additional laundry on Tuesday, increased hours in the office on Wednesday, more school assignments on Thursday, and twice the cleaning on Friday. And if we're going to receive all of Sunday as a God-given day of rest, then Saturday may need to become a day of work too. Every hour we spend doing our ordinary tasks on Monday through Saturday is time we free up to spend with our Lord on his day:

- Spend an extra thirty minutes each day doing small tasks you might be tempted to put off until Sunday.
- Pursue a job schedule that allows you to take Sundays off.[1]

1 Some kinds of labor, what the seventeenth-century Westminster Assembly called "works of necessity and mercy" are unavoidable on

- Make time during the week to go grocery shopping and do other errands.

Prepare Your Body

When I was a college student, I often didn't do a good job of planning for Sabbath rest. Saturday night was when my friends and I would hang out, eat pizza, and watch movies. Sometimes we'd eat at a favorite restaurant before tiptoeing back into the dorm, late and half-sick from sodas and greasy food. I'm ashamed of the number of Sunday mornings my eyelids began to grow heavy during the sermon because I didn't prepare my body the night before.

It may seem counterintuitive that we have to get our bodies ready to rest, but Sabbath rest is about more than a long afternoon nap. To do the work of

---

Sundays. Medical professionals and emergency service workers, for example, may sometimes need to work Sunday shifts. "Westminster Shorter Catechism," in *The Westminster Confession of Faith: Together with the Larger Catechism and the Shorter Catechism with Scripture Proofs*, 3rd ed. (Christian Education & Publications, 1990), q. 60.

worshiping and enjoying God on the Lord's Day, we need to care for our bodies ahead of time. This means we'll make deliberate choices during the week with Sunday in mind:

- Establish a reasonable bedtime on Saturday.
- Turn off your screens early on Saturday to avoid media-induced stress and information overload.

Prepare Your Soul

When Rob and I were dating, in addition to making practical arrangements for his visits, I'd also spend more than a few minutes daydreaming about how wonderful it was going to be to see him again. I'd reread his recent letters to me, and I'd rehearse in my mind all the things he enjoyed so we could make sure to do them together.

In a similar way, our preparations for Sabbath rest involve more than just the practicalities of work and health. They involve our hearts and minds. Puritan Richard Baxter recounted how the young people in his community would meet together on Saturday nights to sing songs of praise and to pray together. He described this practice as allowing them to simply bank their spiritual coals and then turn them over the next day rather than struggling to light a new fire.[2] We, too, keep the coals of Sabbath alive in our hearts when we read God's word, sing praises, pray, and meditate on the goodness of God throughout the week, not just on Sunday:

- Pray during the week for the Lord to meet you in your Sabbath rest.
- On Saturday, read the Scripture text your pastor will preach from the next day.
- If you live with others, have a time of worship on Saturday evening and pray for the Lord to bless you and your church as you gather on Sunday.

2 Jeremy Walker, *Our Chief of Days: The Principle, Purpose, and Practice of the Lord's Day* (Evangelical Press, 2019), 70.

Grace for the Ill-Prepared

Of course, we don't prepare for the Sabbath in our own strength, and we'll never prepare perfectly. Despite our best efforts, there will sometimes be dishes in the sink on Sunday morning, and we won't always wake up eager to worship. The Lord knows this and has compassion on us. The Sabbath was made for people—even people who don't prepare well.

In Acts 20, we read the account of young Eutychus falling asleep on the Lord's Day during Paul's sermon. He may have been a slave who worked long hours beyond his control; he may have been a typical teenager who didn't order his time carefully. Whatever the reason, his drooping eyelids caused him to fall from a window and plunge to his death. His weariness lulled him to sleep, but the Lord's mercy woke him from death and enabled him to return to worship (vv. 9–11). When our own preparations for the Sabbath are lacking, we can humbly ask the Lord to send his Spirit to rouse our sluggish hearts so we can rest in him. It's a gift he loves to give.

Reflection Questions

1. Which of your ordinary activities is the most difficult to set aside for a day? Why?

2. What steps could you take to prepare for Sabbath rest before Sunday?

4

Rest in the Lord

LIKE MANY PEOPLE, you probably have a friend with whom you wish you could spend more time. It's usually that friend who knows you best and loves you anyway, and with whom you have enough history to not have to explain every thing from the beginning. You two talk about how someday soon you're going to have a girls' night out, or maybe even one day go on a road trip together, but life always gets in the way. Until it's on the calendar, you both know it's unlikely to ever happen.

Many of us feel the same about our relationship with Christ. We'd love to spend more time with our soul's dearest friend, but life keeps upending our plans.

Morning Bible reading gets cut short by minor household emergencies, our goals to memorize Scripture more and scroll Instagram less never seem to materialize, and we struggle to find a moment in the day for even a simple prayer or two. Thankfully, the Lord doesn't wait for us to agree on a time to get together that's convenient for both of us. He simply tells us that he's arranged everything, and he'll be showing up every Sunday.

In the previous chapter, we saw that Sabbath rest invites us to clear our calendars of our ordinary activities.[1] Now we see what we can do with one free day every week. Chiefly, we can rest in the Lord—worship him, grow in our knowledge of and love for him, and enjoy him and all his benefits.

Time with the Lord

On the Sabbath, the Lord fulfills our longing to spend more time with him.

1 Our ordinary activities are what the Westminster Confession of Faith calls "worldly employments and recreations." "Westminster Confession of Faith," in *The Westminster Confession of Faith: Together with the Larger Catechism and the Shorter Catechism with Scripture Proofs*, 3rd ed. (Christian Education & Publications, 1990), 21.8.

Worship

The single best thing you can do on Sunday is go to church. In corporate worship, God speaks to us in his word as it is read and preached, and we speak to him in our prayers and songs of praise. If we are to rest in the Lord, we must draw near to him where he is. We should seek to participate in all the Sunday worship gatherings our church holds—morning worship, evening worship, Sunday school, prayer meeting, and small group. We should also make the most of our time in worship, seizing every opportunity to commune with Christ:

- Open your Bible and follow along with the Scripture readings.
- Actively listen to the preaching, taking notes if it helps.
- Say "Amen" to the prayers—either silently or out loud—deliberately engaging with what is being said.
- Sing heartily, offering your praise in faith to the Lord.

Grow

Productivity experts talk about the problem of "decision fatigue," the mental drain from repeatedly having to figure out what to do next. By contrast, humans flourish when we intentionally limit our choices in common situations in order to make the next step obvious, even inevitable. It's easier to squeeze in a walk if you're already wearing sneakers and easier to start dinner if you've already planned the week's menu. Surprisingly small tweaks bring you closer to accomplishing your goals for the day.

Most of us would say that spiritual growth is something we desire, but in a world of seemingly endless choices of what to do with our time, we often fail to pursue this goal. On the Sabbath, though, the Lord helpfully limits our options by declaring work off-limits and worship our priority.

We can also take practical steps to make growing in grace the easy thing to do next. For me, this means something as simple as wearing my church clothes all day as a signal to myself that I'm always ready to worship. It means putting my phone in another room but leaving my Bible and notebook in plain sight so they're easiest to grab. It means filling a shelf with Christian books that I want to read (and a shelf for my kids too). It means viewing every moment of the day as a chance to know Christ more.

Whether you have long quiet hours or just a few minutes during a little one's nap, if you're ready, you'll find opportunities to sit at Jesus's feet and commune with him. They may not seem like much, but over a lifetime of Sundays, these practices cultivate spiritual maturity:

- Read a whole book of the Bible in one sitting. Search online to find which books you can read in the time you have. For example, these each take around fifteen minutes: Joel, Malachi, Philippians, Colossians, 1 Timothy, 1 Thessalonians.[2]

2 See for example "Infographic: You Have More Time for Bible Reading Than You Think," Crossway, November 19, 2018, https://www.crossway.org/.

- Memorize a few Scripture verses; review every Sunday until you know them.
- Read a chapter of a Christian book on a theological topic you've wanted to understand.
- Sing a hymn from the morning's worship service and learn the lyrics.

Delight

The first answer of the Westminster Shorter Catechism famously describes the aim of all human life: "Man's chief end is to glorify God, and to enjoy him forever."[3] Enjoying God sounds like something we'd all want to do, but true enjoyment can't be rushed. (Nobody really enjoys a meal eaten in five minutes while standing at the kitchen counter!) To enjoy our God, we need time to slow down and savor who he is and what he has done. Thankfully, God has given us that time. Delighting in the Lord is both the purpose and promise of Sabbath rest: "If you . . . call the

3 "Westminster Shorter Catechism," in *The Westminster Confession of Faith: Together with the Larger Catechism and the Shorter Catechism with Scripture Proofs*, q. 1.

Sabbath a delight," declares Isaiah, ". . . then you shall take delight in the LORD" (Isa. 58:13–14). When we use the Sabbath to enjoy our God, we will find him endlessly delightful:

- Choose a beautiful truth from Scripture—for example, your salvation, God's holiness, Christ's incarnation—to meditate on for a few minutes. Think about it from every angle you can. Consider its implications for your life. Give thanks to the Lord.
- Go for a walk outside and praise God for the things you see and hear in his creation.
- Make a playlist of psalms, hymns, and worship songs, and savor rich truths set to lovely music.

Rest Until You Rest

The Puritans had a saying, "Pray until you pray," by which they meant that we ought to push through the awkwardness, distractions, and superficiality which can accompany prayer and ought not to give up until we truly cry out to God in our hearts. In the same way, we should "rest until we rest." Taking one whole day for worship and delight in the Lord will probably feel uncomfortable at first. It may be tempting to quit. But when we persist—when we keep showing up on the Lord's Day in the places where he promises to meet us—we'll begin to truly rest in Christ and experience the blessing of his presence.

Reflection Questions

1. What is one way you can make worship with your church a bigger priority on Sunday?

2. What is one way you can minimize decision fatigue on Sunday and make rest in the Lord the easy choice?

5

Rest with the Lord's People

LATE IN HIS LIFE, the apostle John was exiled to the island of Patmos. Nevertheless, he wrote, "I was in the Spirit on the Lord's day" (Rev. 1:10). In a situation in which every day may have seemed like a repeat of the day before, John set aside one day for worship. He also remembered his connection to all God's people, calling himself the "brother" and "partner" of the seven churches to whom he wrote (v. 9). While John was in the Spirit on the Lord's Day on Patmos, he knew his brothers and sisters throughout Asia were likewise worshiping. And the Lord graciously ministered to John by giving him a vision not of solitary communion with Christ but of the corporate worship of "a great multitude that no one could number, from every nation" (Rev. 7:9). Seeing John spending the Sabbath alone, the Lord called to him, "Come up here" (Rev. 4:1), and invited him to join a vast company of saints and angels worshiping before his throne (Rev. 4:1–11).

Likewise, the Lord calls to us on the Lord's Day, draws us out of our spiritual solitude, and brings us among not only his people on earth but also "innumerable angels in festal gathering," "the assembly of the firstborn who are enrolled in heaven," God, "the spirits of the righteous made perfect," and Jesus (Heb. 12:22–24). Sabbath rest isn't merely for resting alone in the Lord. It's for resting with all who also belong to him. It's for resting with the church.

Ways to Rest

Consider several ways to rest with the Lord's people on the Lord's Day.

Worship

Puritan David Clarkson reflected on the blessing of worshiping with the church, explaining, "Public worship is more edifying than private. In private you provide for your own good, but in public you do good both to yourselves and others."[1] When we sing in corporate worship, it points others to Christ (Eph. 5:19; Col. 3:16). When we pray, we bring one another to the throne of grace (Heb. 4:16). When we hear God's word read and preached, we learn together from our gracious Lord (1 Thess. 2:13). As a member of the body of Christ, each person's worship is indispensable to the others, and the others' worship is necessary for each person (1 Cor. 12:12–31).

On Sundays, God's people do good to one another's souls:

- Gather with the church for worship, even if you are on vacation.

1 David Clarkson, "Public Worship to Be Preferred Before Private," in *The Practical Works of David Clarkson* (Edinburgh, 1865), 3:192.

- Sit close to your fellow church members during the service, and rejoice in the privilege of singing, praying, and hearing from God in the company of his people.
- Take a group to visit a church member who is unable to come to worship; read Scripture, sing, and pray together.

Encouragement

Some of my sweetest memories of Sabbath rest are from my time as a college student. Some fellow students and I committed ourselves to setting apart the day—closing our books and laptops and opening our hearts to the Lord and his people. After church, we would often spend Sundays in the homes of hospitable church members. Other times, we gathered in someone's dorm room to listen to and discuss a recorded sermon. It's quite possible that our grades and our social lives suffered as a result. It's certain that our souls did not.

"Let us consider how to stir up one another to love and good works," wrote the author of Hebrews, "not neglecting to meet together, as is the habit of some, but encouraging one another, and all the more as you see the Day drawing near" (Heb. 10:24–25). Gathering with God's people is a vital means of stirring one another up in the life of faith. And though our weekdays are often filled with other obligations, the Lord gives us one day in seven to encourage one another.

- Learn the names of people in your church (even the children!) and greet them with a smile.
- Invite church members for Sunday lunch; as you eat, retell your Christian testimony and ask the people around your table to tell theirs. Rejoice together in the work God has done in your lives.
- Send an email to some missionaries you support, encouraging them that you are coming alongside them in prayer.

Mercy

Jesus is our greatest example of what it means to pursue rest on the Sabbath. As we've already noted, he made participation in corporate worship his habit (Luke 4:16). He spent time with his disciples, encouraging them in the faith (Luke 4:31–32). And he often used some of the day to feed and heal those who were in need (e.g., Matt. 12:1–14). In a day set apart to honor the Lord, we too welcome opportunities to show mercy.

- Give generously when the offering plate is passed, asking God to use your money to help those in need.
- Look for someone in the congregation to ask, "What can I do for you this week?"
- Take a meal or send a card to a church member who is lonely, grieving, or sick.

Put on Your Mittens

In a society increasingly marked by isolation and loneliness, Sabbath rest provides an opportunity for us to gather with other believers for our spiritual good. I love the illustration from one writer who used the example of a woolen mitten. Throughout the week, believers are like the separated fingers in a glove—working independently but prone to growing cold. On the Sabbath, though, we come together, and the vitality of each one makes the others warm.[2]

"I was glad," the psalmist sang, "when they said to me, 'Let us go to the house of the LORD!' " (Ps. 122:1). Week after week, this corporate invitation is our joy too. On the Lord's Day, we rest with the Lord's people.

Reflection Questions

1. Who is one person you could encourage this Sunday? How?

2. What is one thing from this booklet that has changed the way you think about Sabbath rest?

3. What is one thing from this booklet that you'd like to put into regular practice?

2 Lewis O. Thompson, *The Prayer Meeting and Its Improvement*, 5th ed. (Chicago, 1878), 231.

Conclusion

IN THE PERIOD DRAMA *Downton Abbey*, the elderly dowager countess struggles to adapt to a changing English society. When another character mentions his weekly schedule, she asks in genuine puzzlement, "What is a 'weekend'?"[1] We chuckle because a "weekend" is ingrained in our contemporary life and needs no explanation. It's the two days when we are free from the demands of our day jobs and get to do what we want.

Or is it?

In his instructions about the Sabbath, the Lord asks us to consider our schedules with the fresh eyes

1 *Downton Abbey*, season 1, episode 2, "Episode Two," written by Julian Fellowes, directed by Ben Bolt, aired October 3, 2010, on ITV.

of someone not schooled by the expectations or priorities of our neighbors. He calls us to examine whether we could (and should!) submit our time, our work, our loyalties, and our aims to him. And he invites us to see whether there might be blessing along his narrow way. "Come to me, all who labor and are heavy laden," Jesus says, "and I will give you rest. Take my yoke upon you, and learn from me, for I am gentle and lowly in heart, and you will find rest for your souls. For my yoke is easy, and my burden is light" (Matt. 11:28–29).

As we've seen, setting aside one day in seven is a yoke of sorts. It requires us to give up our own desires and goals, it prescribes our actions and agendas, and it may prevent us from material gain. And yet the Lord invites us to rest in this yoke—to take the day he has given to us and find him sweeter and his ways more delightful than anything the world can offer.

Come to him and rest.

Recommended Resources

Arand, Charles P., Craig L. Blomberg, Skip MacCarty, and Joseph A. Pipa. *Perspectives on the Sabbath: Four Views*. Edited by Christopher John Donato. B&H, 2011.

This book provides a helpful overview of the major Christian perspectives on the Sabbath. Among the four authors, Joseph Pipa makes the case for the first day of the week as the Christian Sabbath and for the practice of Sabbath rest as a moral obligation for believers today.

Pang, Alex Soojung-Kim. *Rest: Why You Get More Done When You Work Less*. Basic Books, 2018.

If we believe God made and ordered the world in concert with his commandments, it shouldn't be surprising that scientific study bears out the biblical truth of our need for periodic, deliberate rest. Researcher Alex Pang prescribes such rest as if it were a novel idea, but Christian readers can see the fingerprint of God in this book's findings.

Tripp, Paul David. *Sunday Matters: 52 Devotionals to Prepare Your Heart for Church*. Crossway, 2024.

With readings for a whole year, Paul Tripp's book helps individuals and families make the most of Sundays. Each week's reflections, suggested Scripture readings, and prompts for discussion take the guesswork out of how to rest in the Lord on his day.

Walker, Jeremy. *Our Chief of Days: The Principle, Purpose, and Practice of the Lord's Day*. Evangelical Press, 2019.

Although Sabbath practices are often misunderstood as being dour and legalistic, they are actually the path of joy for Christians. Jeremy Walker, pastor of Maidenbower Baptist Church, explores what the Bible says about the Lord's Day and gives readers warm, practical counsel for how to benefit from that day.